The Essential Buyer's Guide

JAGUAR

XK8 & XKR

1996-2005

Your marque expert:
Nigel Thorley

T0386780

VELOCE PUBLISHING
THE PUBLISHER OF FINE AUTOMOTIVE BOOKS

www.veloce.co.uk

First published in April 2011, reprinted January 2014, May 2015 and November 2017 by Veloce Publishing Limited, Veloce House, Parkway Farm Business Park, Middle Farm Way, Poundbury, Dorchester, Dorset, DT1 3AR, England.
Fax 01305 250479/e-mail info@veloce.co.uk/web www.veloce.co.uk or www.velocebooks.com.
ISBN: 978-1-845843-59-5 UPC: 6-36847-04359-9
Readers with ideas for automotive books, or books on other transport or related hobby subjects, are invited to write to the editorial director of Veloce Publishing at the above address.
British Library Cataloguing in Publication Data – A catalogue record for this book is available from the British Library.
Typesetting, design and page make-up all by Veloce Publishing Ltd on Apple Mac. Printed and bound by CPI Group (UK) Ltd, Croydon, CR0 4YY.

Introduction
– the purpose of this book

The launch of the XK8 in 1996 heralded a new beginning for Jaguar Cars. After the demise of the E-type in 1974 the company moved away from the two-seater rakish sports car image, to touring in the grand style with the XJ-S, a model that stayed in production longer than any previous sporting Jaguar.

Ford's 1989 take-over saw vital cash pumped into Jaguar Cars, strengthening the model range and production quality. Ford's first priority was a new saloon (X-300) as a volume seller, while it cancelled Jaguar's own ill-conceived replacement for the XJ-S (the XJ41 or F-type).

The key to Jaguar's re-birth was an entirely new V8 engine (AJ-V8), replacing both the inefficient, expensive-to-build V12, and the somewhat unrefined multi-valve straight-six (AJ6/16). Previously, all new Jaguar engines debuted in a sporting model – and it was to be no different for the 4.0-litre 290bhp V8.

Launched in September 1996 the AJ-V8 appeared in Jaguar's new sporting model, the XK8, an interesting and intuitive collaboration of existing and new technology. Although very much a grand tourer, the XK8 reintroduced some of the passion felt for the E-type, with a curvaceous body and strikingly similar nose treatment to the 1960s icon. Beneath the new skin lay the foundations of the good-old XJ-S architecture in the floorpan, limiting some of the changes the designers would have wished to make.

Retaining Jaguar tradition, the interior was beautifully presented with the usual combination of veneer and leather, but with contemporary options. Coupé and Convertible models were available from the start, the latter with well-designed power operated hood; one of the few 'rag-tops' that looked good with the top up!

Mechanically, as well as the new ultra-refined V8 engine, came a new ZF automatic transmission, and front and rear suspension.

Receiving world acclaim, the XK8 was followed by the introduction of Jaguar's first supercharged production sports car, the XKR (1998 onward), and a continual programme of enhancements, modifications, and special editions during the model's nine-year production run.

The XK8 re-established the Jaguar tradition of fine sporting cars; so much so that in its relatively brief production run, more of these models were produced, pro rata, than any other. Today, it still has a very strong following, and it won't be long before the XK follows the trend of other Jaguar sporting models, becoming an icon, almost in its own time. There has never been a better time to consider buying an XK8, with plenty of choice and superb value for money. Enjoy!

Thanks

My personal thanks to all those who have contributed to this publication, in particular David Marks for his technical expertise.

Contents

Essential Buyer's Guide™ currency
At the time of publication a BG unit of currency "●" equals approximately
£1.00/US$1.32/Euro 1.12. Please adjust to suit current exchange rates.

Ample, but not excessive, foot and legroom for very tall drivers.

Tall and short drivers
The XK8 was built around the XJ-S floorpan and seat frames, so there isn't a great deal of seat movement, meaning legroom is limited. Very tall drivers will notice that headroom is only just adequate.

Weight of controls
Light and easy to handle, all having power assisted steering and brakes. The handbrake is not ideally situated, being between the driver's seat and door. It operates in the opposite way to other modern cars, too, and always rests flat to the carpet (whether it's applied or not!).

Will it fit in the garage?
Length: 187in (4750mm)
Width: 72in (1829mm)
Height: 51in (1295mm)

Interior space
Although a 2+2, the rear seat is only suitable for young children, and legroom is even worse with the later models with thicker front seatbacks. Headroom at the front is 'adequate,' but there's

Rear seat accommodation is only suitable for young children.

plenty of elbow room, with most front seat occupants finding these cars very comfortable.

Luggage capacity
The XK8 was designed to take the obligatory two sets of golf clubs, so there's more space than in many saloons. The spare wheel and battery don't intrude, and fitted luggage is available.

Interior accommodation is restricted to a centre console cubby area, a reasonable glovebox, and door pockets.

Boot space is excellent: best in class.

Running costs
The V8 engines are quite economical, and 26mpg should easily be achievable, more with the later 4.2-litre. Normal servicing costs are not high, with 10,000 mile intervals, but extra maintenance on items like gearbox oil/filter changes can rake up the bills considerably. Diagnosing problems without specialist equipment can be an issue for the DIY mechanic.

Usability
A practical car in all conditions.

Parts availability
Nearly everything is still available or accessible through the many specialists around. Good tested used parts can also be acquired.

Parts cost
Although still a relatively modern car, and a lot of parts are still available from Jaguar, it is surprising how many items are now out of stock, and may not be remanufactured, due to loss of tooling, cost implications, etc. Future availability will much depend on popularity and the necessity to keep the vehicles on the road, rather than the need to keep items, such as trim, available.

Overall parts supply at present is still good for most items, although some are being remade and therefore are expensive, but, in the main, XK parts are still cheaper than those for other contemporary vehicles of the same calibre

Insurance
Insurance costs can be cheaper than you might think. Being a member of a Jaguar club can enable access to specialist schemes, with discounts for limited use, multiple vehicles, etc.

Investment potential
Already showing signs of price rises, but only for special edition models and those cars in exceptionally good condition.

Alternatives
Rivals are the Mercedes SL, BMW 6 Series, and Lexus Coupé. The Maserati is a strong contender, as is the Aston Martin DB7, but the XK8 wins-out on cost and refinement.

2 Cost considerations
– affordable, or a money pit?

Purchase price
Buying the best car you can afford is certainly true with the XK. The buyer must consider the amount of work that may be necessary to put a cheap car into good order.

A service history is vital, although these days not necessarily with a franchised dealership. A fully stamped-up service book is a good sign but look for proof that the work has actually been done. Never take an XK on face value, as there are hidden issues that could cost a lot of money to rectify.

Servicing
Typical intervals are:
Regular service   10,000 miles
Renew sparkplugs   20,000 miles

Renew air filter   30,000 miles
                        (20,000 XKR)
Major service   60,000 miles

Parts price (approximate)
Brake pads (front): x68
Brake pads (front, Brembo R-Performance): x250
Brake discs (front): x190
Brake discs (front, Brembo R-Performance): x410
Brake pads (rear): x42
Brake pads (rear, Brembo R-Performance): x250
Brake discs (rear): x168
Brake discs (rear, Brembo R-Performance): x410
Engine top timing chain tensioners: x57
Water pump: x96
Thermostat: x31
Front shock absorbers: x128

Front shock absorbers (CATS): x183
Front shock absorbers (R-Performance): x220
Rear shock absorbers: x141
Rear shock absorbers (CATS): x189
Rear shock absorbers (R-Performance): x210
Wheel bearings: x46
Rear bumper bar mounts: x36
Top wishbone bushes: x30
Headlamp unit: x429
Heading HID Xenon: x750

Used parts
In ready supply but ensure they are tested before purchase. Many refurbished parts now also available.

Buy the best you can afford, it's cheaper in the long run.

So many XKs were produced that there's a good supply of used, good condition parts to keep costs down.

3 Living with an XK
– will you get along together?

Great looks and practicality.

Good points
Good looks.
Refinement.
Ride and handling.
Smooth V8 engine.
Performance and
economy.
Luxurious interior.
Big boot.
Prestige.
Good support back-up.

Bad points
Body/paint vulnerability
to minor damage/paint
chips.
Corrosion areas around
floorpan.
Rear seat
accommodation.
Early engine problems.
Regular maintenance
vital (including areas like
gearboxes).
Some replacement parts
can be very expensive.

Summary
A beautifully styled, very
capable car that's a
great drive. Reasonably
economical, but you need
to buy the best you can
afford to guard against
costly upkeep.

Not much in the tool kit, but a well maintained example
won't need it!

Models

The model range is quite simple: two body styles (Coupé and Convertible); two engine sizes, 4.0-litre and 4.2-litre; normally-aspirated or supercharged.

Nearly double the number of Convertibles were made compared to Coupés, and they're still the more costly of the two to purchase. Supercharged models equated to only about one-third of total production, and the earlier 4.0-litre engines were more popular than the later 4.2-litre versions.

Early XK8 Coupé with standard 17in Revolver wheels.

For practical and regular use the Coupé wins: cheaper to buy; better visibility; more assured security because of the 'tin top;' and many people prefer the styling.

The Convertible is ideal for use on high days and holidays. The lined hood is fully retractable and seals well against the elements. The only downside is the hand fitting of the hood cover, competitors like the Mercedes SL have a self-closing metal panel. However, the XK benefits from a bigger boot because of this.

Early XK8 Convertible with 18in Flute wheels.

9

Unique interior treatment for US Portfolio special edition.

Body-wise the cars remained virtually identical until the last facelift in 2004, with relatively minor styling alterations.

Several special editions were produced, starting with the Silverstone (painted silver) in 2000, and the XKR 100 in 2001 (painted black). The Carbon Fibre was produced In 2004, with its unique dashboard treatment, and there were special editions for the US market – the XKR Portfolio (blue or red) with special interior finishes.

The final factory special editions were to commemorate the end of production in 2005; the S model in the UK and Europe, and the Victory in the US.

Values

As is usually the case, the largest part of a car's perceived value is down to its condition, regardless of model. However, in the case of the XK, as production only finished in 2005, and so many cars are still in the hands of their original owners, normal depreciation still applies.

Obviously the older the car the cheaper the price, but values will vary dramatically according to mileage and history. Convertibles and supercharged models remain the most expensive. Equipment levels will also affect price, so items like the Premium Sound System, 19in or 20in alloy wheels, Adaptive Cruise Control, etc, will add value. Earlier models were also available with a choice of interior trim packages – 'Classic' (all-leather and walnut veneer), and 'Sport' (half leather and dark-stained maple woodwork), the latter being less popular and less valuable.

It's very difficult to devise a pricing structure, but given that all things are equal relating to trim and equipment levels, the following percentages provide a rough guide.

Facelift S/Victory **100%**
Special Editions **90%**
Mid-term XKR Convertibles **90%**
Mid-term XK8 Convertibles **80%**
Mid-term XKR Coupés **80%**
Mid-term XK8 Coupés **75%**
Early XKR Convertibles **60%**
Early XK8 Convertibles **55%**
Early XKR Coupés **55%**
Early XKR Coupés **50%**

Compare pre-facelift model (left) and last-of-the-line.

5 Before you view
– be well informed

To avoid a wasted journey, be very clear about what questions you want to ask before you pick up the telephone. Some of these points might appear basic, but when you're excited about the prospect of buying your dream classic, it's amazing how some of the most obvious things slip the mind. Also, check car magazines for the current values of the model you're interested in, which give both a price guide and auction results.

Where is the car?
Is it going to be worth travelling to the next county, state, or even another country? A locally advertised car, although it may not sound very interesting, can add to your knowledge for very little effort, so make a visit – it might even be in better condition than expected.

View private sale cars at the owners' premises.

Dealer or private sale?
Establish early on if the car is being sold by its owner or by a trader. A private owner should have all the history, so don't be afraid to ask detailed questions.

A dealer may have more limited knowledge of a car's history, but should have some documentation. A dealer may offer a warranty/guarantee (ask for a printed copy) and finance.

Cost of collection and delivery?
A dealer may well be used to quoting for delivery by car transporter. A private owner may agree to meet you halfway, but only agree to this after you have seen the car at the vendor's address to validate the documents. Conversely, you could meet halfway and agree the sale, but insist on meeting at the vendor's address for the handover.

View – when and where?
It's always preferable to view at the vendors home or business premises. In the case of a private sale, the car's documentation should tally with the vendor's name and address. Arrange to view only in daylight and avoid a wet day: most cars look better in poor light or when wet.

Reason for sale?
Do make this one of the first questions. Why is the car being sold, and how long has it been with the current owner? How many previous owners?

Left-hand drive to right-hand drive/specials and convertibles?

It's unlikely that an XK will have been converted from left- to right-hand drive, but do check the origin of the car. With new cars exported around the world, detail specifications changed and in, some cases, even lights had to comply with specific markets which, when a car is exported to another country, means that such detail specifications have to be changed to meet regulations.

Condition (body/chassis/interior/mechanicals)?

Ask for an honest appraisal of the car's condition. Ask specifically about some of the check items described in chapter 7.

All original specification?

An original equipment car is invariably of higher value than a customised version.

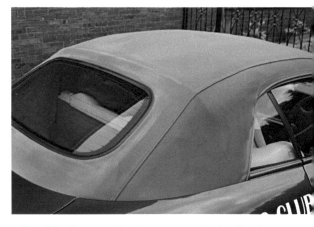

Condition is everything, but an owner's view is often biased.

Matching data/legal ownership?

Do VIN/chassis, engine numbers, and license plate match the official registration document? Is the owner's name and address recorded in the official registration documents?

For those countries that require an annual test of roadworthiness, does the car have a document showing it complies (an MoT certificate in the UK)?

If a smog/emissions certificate is mandatory, does the car have one?

If required, does the car carry a current road fund licence/licence plate tag?

Cars are customised to personal taste, not necessarily yours!

Does the vendor own the car outright? Money might be owed to a finance company or bank: the car could even be stolen. Several organisations will supply

the data on ownership, based on the car's licence plate number, for a fee. Such companies can often also tell you whether the car has been 'written-off' by an insurance company. In the UK the following organisations can supply vehicle data:
HPI – 01722 422 422
AA – 0870 600 0836
DVLA – 0870 240 0010
RAC – 0870 533 3660
Other countries will have similar organisations.

Signs of a proud and careful owner, like the plastic boot floor cover.

Insurance?

Check with your existing insurer before setting out; your current policy might not cover you to drive the car if you do purchase it.

How you can pay

A cheque will take several days to clear, and the seller may prefer to sell to a cash buyer. However, a banker's draft (a cheque issued by a bank) is as good as cash, but safer, so contact your own bank and become familiar with the formalities that are necessary to obtain one.

Buying at auction?

If the intention is to buy at auction see chapter 10 for further advice.

Professional vehicle check (mechanical examination)?

There are marque/model specialists who will undertake a professional examination of a vehicle on your behalf. Owners' clubs will be able to put you in touch with such specialists.

Other organisations that will carry out a general professional check in the UK are:
AA – 0800 085 3007
ABS – 0800 358 5855
RAC – 0870 533 3660
Again, other countries will have organisations offering similar services.

Never agree to view a car in the rain, as water droplets can hide problems.

Before you rush out of the door, gather together a few items that will help as you work your way around the car.

The proper equipment, used safely, can help you to **more thoroughly check a car.**

This book
This book is designed to be your guide at every step, so take it along and use the check boxes to help you assess each area of the car you're interested in. Don't be afraid to let the seller see you using it.

Reading glasses (if you need them for close work)
Take your reading glasses if you need them to read documents and make close up inspections.

Magnet (not powerful, a fridge magnet is ideal)
A magnet will help you check if the car is full of filler from previous, cheap repairs. Use the magnet to sample bodywork areas all around the car, but be careful not to damage the paintwork. Expect to find a little filler here and there, but not whole panels.

Torch
A torch with fresh batteries will be useful for peering into the wheelarches and under the car.

Probe (a small screwdriver works very well)

A small screwdriver can be used – with care – as a probe, particularly on the underside. With this you should be able to check any areas of severe corrosion, but be careful – if it's really bad the screwdriver might go right through the metal!

Overalls

Be prepared to get dirty. Take along a pair of overalls, if you have them.

Mirror on a stick

Fixing a mirror at an angle on the end of a stick may seem odd, but you'll probably need it to check the condition of the underside of the car. It will also help you to peer into some of the important crevices. You can also use it, together with the torch, along the underside of the sills and on the floor. You're looking for accident damage, as well as corrosion.

Digital camera

If you have the use of a digital camera, take it along so that later you can study some areas of the car more closely. Take a picture of any part of the car that causes you concern, and seek a friend's opinion.

A friend, preferably a knowledgeable enthusiast

Ideally, have a friend or knowledgeable enthusiast accompany you: a second opinion is always valuable.

A digital camera provides instant results – you can review after inspecting the car.

A knowledgeable XK enthusiast can help a great deal when checking an intended buy.

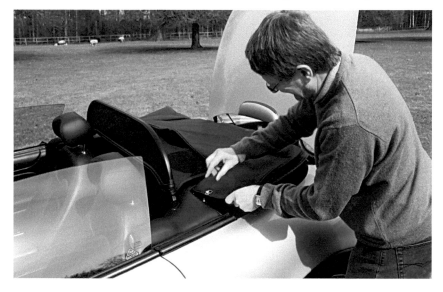

Road test

Assuming you have adequate insurance cover, it's vital you road test any car you're considering purchasing. This should be agreed with the owner prior to viewing, asking him, if practical, not to warm the engine, thus allowing you to start it from cold.

In the driver's seat, ensure all the controls you need work correctly, including electric seat adjustment, steering wheel and mirror adjustment. Turn on the ignition and allow the car to cycle. Drop the driver's window, so you can hear the engine as you start it: listen for any rattles or other noises from the engine area, or for blows from the exhaust system. Engine rattles on start-up could be attributable to timing chain issues. If the engine sounds 'flat' when starting this could just be due to a poor battery, but it could be the start of the Nikasil lining in the bores breaking up (a common problem on pre-2000 engines).

A quick glance in the rear view mirror should show any haze or blue smoke coming from the exhaust, which should never be a problem with these engines if maintained properly. Check the instrument visual read-out for error messages, warning lights, etc. Disregard the auxiliary gauges (except fuel) as they are generally accepted as 'comfort' instruments, and don't provide sufficiently useful information.

The engine should tick over smoothly and quietly. Rev the engine, again listening for unusual noises or hesitation from the throttle indicating problems to be investigated. Normally-aspirated cars have variable valve timing (VVT). If the engine is smooth and quiet upon

A road test over varying conditions is a must when considering an XK.

Dry dust and dirt isn't anything to be frightened of.

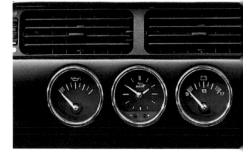

The most accurate auxiliary gauge is the clock!

Test all the gear positions.

starting, when revving to 1200rpm you should hear a distinct 'click' to indicate the VVT coming into operation. If, however, the engine takes on a rhythmic ticking when cold, this could indicate wear in the VVT units: not a major issue at this point, but they will eventually need replacing.

Selecting Drive, there should be no strong judder as the transmission engages. At this point check the handbrake is adjusted sufficiently to hold the car when in gear. Moving off, the car should run smoothly, with almost imperceptible gear changes. Now is the time to put the driver's window up and listen for unacceptable wind noise (even the Convertibles should be virtually noise free) and for unwarranted knocks and rattles through the car from steering, suspension or drive train.

Models like the XKR, and others fitted with 'sport' suspension and 19in or 20in wheels, will give a harder ride, yet there should be no knocks or bumps from the suspension indicating worn bushes, shock absorbers or even springs. The brakes should be smooth and progressive, and a little harder if the car is fitted with the larger Brembo items. Judder is normally due to warped or corroded discs which will not be cheap to replace. Steering should be precise with little free play, but watch for wander. Tramlining can affect cars with softer bushes and lower profile tyres.

Damaged wheels can prove expensive to repair or replace.

Try all the normal operating controls, like cruise control if fitted, air-conditioning, and audio systems, all of which could be expensive to fix. Check all the auxiliary controls work properly, like window motors and interior lighting.

Finally, if a Convertible, check that the hood mechanism works. Many earlier cars suffered from congealing fluid, necessitating complete purging and replacement.

Try to drive the car on a variety of road surfaces and at differing speeds to test for wind noise, wheel balance, and overall smoothness. Ideally, a 20 mile round trip is the best option to get a real 'feel' for the car. It's also worth stopping on occasion, switching off the engine, and re-starting it again, looking for blue smoke behind, rattles, or any hesitancy in starting, all of which indicate problems to be investigated. Cycle through the gears to establish the changes take place correctly and smoothly, and also check that 'Sport' mode is operational.

All extra fitted equipment should be tried. Anything that doesn't work may affect other equipment in the car.

Checks back at base

Once you've identified anything that you want to investigate, return to base and check other areas.

General condition

The advantage of the XK range is that, in many cases, they were purchased as second cars, so will not have been abused or have high mileage. Older cars may have passed through several owners, and their upkeep will have depended on financial considerations as much as care.

Engine bay

With the engine still running, and 'Park' selected, open the bonnet and look around the engine bay for any apparent fluid leaks. Listen for uneven tickover or unusual noises. Switch on the air-conditioning to full cold, and listen for a 'click' as the compressor starts. Ensure it lowers the temperature promptly, feeling the air coming from the vents inside the car. Whilst under the bonnet, check for damaged hoses, clips, and general condition indicating poor maintenance. The engine bay area doesn't have to be totally clean: if the car has been in regular use, it will have naturally gained a fair amount of road grime, and people (including dealerships) are often wary of steam cleaning because of the high density of electronics present in the engine bay.

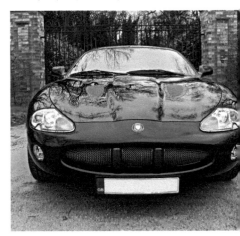

The nose area is the most vulnerable part of the bodywork.

External bodywork

The quality of factory bodywork preparation was very good, so unless a car has been severely damaged, panel gaps, fit, and finish should be excellent. At the front, check the nose section: it's particularly vulnerable to stone chips, which can also penetrate far up the bonnet. The nose is a plastic sub-structure and is often a slightly different colour to the rest of the car, when viewed from certain angles – this is normal.

It's worth checking the condition of the headlight units as they can crack or be affected by condensation, and they are expensive to replace – particularly HID lighting systems. If the car is equipped with a wash-wipe system, check that it works.

The grey painted windscreen surround is also vulnerable to stone chips, and corrosion from ingress of water, and if badly damaged, it must be replaced, which may involved removing the screen. Check the screen for stone chips or other damage; it's expensive to replace, particularly if graduated-tinted or heated.

From the side, the lower sill area is finished with a stone chip crackle finish,

Condensation in the headlamp units is a common problem.

The windscreen surround is another common stone chip area.

Sill join is a common area of stress and paint cracks.

so check for paint peeling from the constant splash of dirt and grime. The exposed flange where outer sill meets inner sill is prone to paint chipping and minor corrosion. Also, check the exposed weld area two-thirds of the way along the sill, where flexing eventually causes the paint to crack. The rear wheelarches are vulnerable to collecting dirt and grime, particularly the exposed lip that wraps around from the sill area. Regular cleaning here prevents dirt building and corrosion starting, but many owners don't bother! Corrosion also affects the rear wing area where it meets the wrap-around bumper. All these areas are easy to identify without detailed inspection.

At the rear, the whole bumper section can become detached due to corrosion of the mounting bolts; steel, within an aluminium thread – a natural recipe for disaster! The mountings are cheap to buy, but if the bolts corrode first, allowing the bumper bar to drop, the cost of replacement can be horrendous.

All these cars were equipped with alloy wheels, varying from 17in to 20in. Many of these are now cheap to replace but, nevertheless, can be an unnecessary expense if the existing ones have not been cared for. Check for damage from kerb scuffing, corrosion from hot brake dust, missing centre caps, and missing or damaged locking wheel nuts. Rectifying scuffed rims isn't an inexpensive job, particularly if they're split type rims, and centre caps are cheap to replace. Locking wheel nuts have to be purchased in sets – not cheap.

Check the tyres. An XK should NEVER be shod with unknown brands, remoulds, or tyres over six years old. Pirelli, Dunlop and Continental were recognised suppliers, but other well known brands are perfectly acceptable. They're not cheap to replace. Remember that on XKR models, and some later XK8s, the rear wheels and tyres are larger than the front. Some unscrupulous traders have been known to fit the same wheels all-round, or even fit the correct wheels the wrong way round (all tyres from 18in and above fitted to these cars were asymmetric, so must be fitted the right way round).

As a final quick check, it's worth standing back and checking both sides of the car, particularly noting any colour difference in panels indicating earlier damage. These are quite large cars and properly done remedial paintwork can cost a lot of money.

Stand well back from the car: you should be able to spot any discolouration indicative of damage repair.

Interior

The interiors generally last very well. The usual places to watch are the driver's seat bolster, which, with constant rubbing, getting in and out of the car, can deteriorate, requiring a new leather panel to be inserted and suitably dyed. Half leather seats are not as desirable and don't wear as well.

Check the veneer in the woodwork as many older cars, or those that

The driver's seat is the first area to suffer wear and tear.

have been subjected to hot climates, will show cracking, particularly around the edge of the instruments. It's almost cheaper to replace all the wood than attempt a minor repair!

Some trim items easily show wear and tear: centre console lids suffer, as do areas around the glove box lid, discolouring particularly.

It's worth checking the carpets, particularly the driver's side, as most are a light colour so mark easily. The hood lining (Convertibles) is vulnerable to discolouration, particularly if left down without the hood cover fitted. Also, check the hood inside and outside for scuffs, tears or discolouration. A replacement hood is much more expensive than you might imagine! The headlining in Coupé models is of lesser concern but worth checking for physical damage, particularly if the rear seating has been used (lack of headroom!).

Boot

Boot areas were hardly ever used so you'll be hard-pressed to find a car with a boot area in poor condition.

However, check that the boot trim carpet is in good condition, particularly the right-hand section which is removed to gain access to the battery and electronics. Bad scuffing, marks or even discolouration (or possibly a change of panel) indicates constant removal.

There should be no signs of exposed wiring, or trim not fitting properly, also indicating that someone has 'been there before.' Remove both the carpeted boot panels to reveal the spare wheel/battery area. Many cars were equipped with a space saver: it's not possible to accommodate one of the larger 19in or 20in alloys in these boots. Is the spare in good condition? Is it correct for the model? Are the tools intact, particularly the locking wheel nut adapter. What condition is the battery in? It lasts a long time and doesn't leak, but once near the end of its life, it will prevent the car functioning properly and is expensive to replace. Are all the electrics in place and not tampered with?

Dependent on equipment level, the boot area will also contain satellite navigation equipment, CD player, Premium Sound amplifier, etc, all of which should be undamaged.

The major areas of concern when checking the condition of an XK8/XKR are the engine, the drive train, and the monocoque floorpan

Early engines were renowned for problems with the Nikasil linings.

Engines

AJ-V8 engines are generally long-lived, and some are easily surviving well into the 200-300,000 mile range with regular and preventative maintenance. However, the earlier 4.0-litre engines fitted to XK8 and XKR models from 1996 to 2000 (VIN Nos 001036 to 042775) were fitted with Nikasil cylinder bore linings which – with fuel's high sulphur level, and irregular use (short, low mileage, cold stop/start driving) – commonly degraded over time. If looking to buy one of these earlier examples you should carry out certain checks covered in chapter 9.

There are other important issues with the AJ-V8 engines – the timing chain tensioners are prone to cracking, and water pumps to failing – all covered in the next chapter.

Reconditioned gearboxes don't come cheap, so beware of faults.

Gearboxes

The XKs were equipped with three types of automatic transmission: the ZF 5HP 24 5-speed unit for the normally-aspirated 4.0-litre engine cars; the Mercedes WSA 580 5-speed unit for the 4.0-litre XKR models; and the ZF 6HP 26 6-speed gearbox from 2002 for all 4.2-litre engined variants. All these gearboxes are supposedly sealed for life so, often, have not had any work carried out on them. But, for longevity, all need regular oil and filter changes, and it's strongly suggested that such servicing is determined from the car's documentation, or that the work is carried out as soon as possible: again, this may affect the final price you pay.

Suspension, steering & brakes

The XK uses a unique and expensive aluminium front suspension subframe, so it's worth checking its condition. Also, front wheel bearings are a serious issue if noisy. At the rear, check for worn shock absorbers (difficult to replace).

The braking system is little different to any other modern, all-round-disc equipped car, but parts can be particularly expensive if the larger and more efficient sporting systems are fitted.

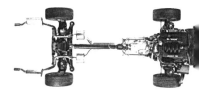

There are lots of suspension and brake issues with a poorly maintained car.

Floorpan

As the XK floorpan is based on the XJ-S, itself derived from the earliest XJ saloons from 1968, it's prone to corrosion areas that need checking.

9 Serious evaluation
– 60 minutes for years of enjoyment

Score each section according to the values in the boxes: 4 = excellent; 3 = good; 2 = average; 1 = poor. Major items have higher values, shown in the relevant boxes. The totting up procedure is detailed at the end of the chapter. Be realistic in your marking!

You've got this far, so now it's time to go for the step-by-step detailed inspection, before deciding whether to part with your hard earned cash. Read, digest, check against your intended purchase and then tick the appropriate box (excellent, good, average or poor) and total the points. Be vigilant over the key pointers first highlighted in chapter 8.

Engine   ☑4 ☑3 ☑2 ☑1

If considering a pre-2001 model year XK, check for a Nikasil engine, and if so, what condition is it in? Steps to help you determine this:

Plate identifying a genuine Jaguar exchange engine.

• Identify the engine number on the log sheet (and on the engine) to see if they match, and if so, does it coincide with a Nikasil-lined number? The first steel-lined AJ-V8 engine (non-Nikasil) was produced in August 2000, with engine No 0008181043. Therefore, that number and any subsequently numbered engine definitely has a steel lining, and Nikasil doesn't apply. However, bear in mind that although steel lined engines were produced from August 2000, some cars later than VIN No 042775 assembled AFTER August 2000 may still have a Nikasil engine, as Jaguar used up their stocks.

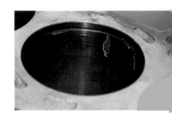

Bad scoring and breaking up of the Nikasil coating in an early engine.

• If a Nikasil engine has been replaced, it normally carried a specific 'Genuine Jaguar Exchange Product' tag mounted on the crankcase, at the rear of the right-hand cylinder head (although this isn't always the case). These engines are now also being rebuilt by a few specialists. Whatever the case, documentation should prove that the engine has been rebuilt or replaced.

• If the car is still fitted with an original Nikasil engine, in most cases, after all this time, a problem isn't likely, particularly if the car has done an average or high mileage. It may also be that the current owner is not aware of, or cannot confirm with documentation, that the engine has been investigated or replaced. In such cases it's vital you have the engine checked before purchasing.

• The principle symptoms of a Nikasil engine problem are poor starting, sluggish performance, and/or piston slap type rattles on start-up. A quick check can be made by removing the air filter assembly: if oil has contaminated this area, this can positively identify the problem.

• For peace of mind have a blow-by (airflow) test carried out on the engine by a specialist. This registers the flow of air in metres per minute, compared to the

Carrying out a blow-by test on an early XK engine.

factory data. A figure between 9 and 19 litres per minute is about normal, and any figure above 30 is suspect. These tests shouldn't be expensive, and the seller should accept the cost.

The next important area of the engine to check is the timing chain tensioners which, in all V8 engines up to the end of 2001/early 2002 build, will have been built with plastic tensioners. These may have started to break down, upsetting the timing of the engine. If not addressed, they ultimately break, causing the engine to completely fail with disastrous results.

An example of top timing chain tensioner degradation.

The upper timing chain tensioners are the main culprits: over time, the stresses of tension and release cause cracks, and then breaks. Jaguar later devised a new style of plastic tensioner, which also tended to give problems in service. Another much sturdier metal type was then devised, and subsequently fitted to all new engines from the 4.2-litre, and to some later genuine Jaguar exchange engines.

Various timing chain tensioners used by Jaguar; the latest is the metal one on the left-hand side.

The problem now is identifying which engines have the revised metal tensionsers fitted from new, which have had them replaced in service, and which still carry the old style plastic types. Unless documentation confirms their replacement with metal tensioners, the only sure way is to remove the cam covers to reveal the tensioners. If still plastic, these should be changed sooner rather than later, and some financial consideration should be made with the price of the car. These can be changed in situ without removing the timing chains so it is not an overly expensive job.

There are still the lower tensioners to consider, which are not accessible to view. Although significantly more reliable, when they fail the engine will produce a pronounced rattling, at which point the lower tensioners and plastic dampers must be replaced – a full day's job!

Having checked these major issues affecting mainly earlier engines, the rest is plain sailing. Check the overall condition of the engine and bay, looking for leaks, condition of coolant hoses, pipework, and wiring. Have there been any apparent fluid leaks? Has the engine recently been thoroughly cleaned? If so, look in the places where it was difficult to clean, for signs of leaks. Check that the oil on the dipstick is clean and uncontaminated. Check the condition and

Check the condition of the drivebelts at the front of the engine: these should be changed regularly.

The V8 throttle body.

tightness of the drivebelt which, according to service schedules, should be changed every 60,000 miles. It has an extensive run around several pulleys. There's also an additional belt on the supercharged models.

V8 engines should run smoothly, but are very complex. Any hesitancy in throttle response is a sign of issues – which could be anything from a faulty sensor to the throttle body. Throttle bodies eventually clog up, leading to the engine cutting-out then re-starting again without issue; a sure sign that the body needs removing, dismantling, and thoroughly cleaning. Indeed, Jaguar Cars replaced many of these throttle bodies in service when the cars were still in production.

The supercharged models are just as reliable, overall. You may experience some rumble from the supercharger bearings, but this is acceptable, and parts are not that expensive to replace (even a complete supercharger), but rarely required.

These engines are not known for oil leaks, but most come from around the cam cover areas where they mate with the heads, or from the plug holes. Whenever the top-end is worked on (like changing the top timing chain tensioners), the seals and cam cover gaskets should be changed; a sign of good preventive maintenance.

Don't be frightened by the thought of superchargers.

The grip clips used on XK hoses often blow off, causing coolant leaks.

Cooling system

The cooling system on AJ-V8 engines is quite complex and highly efficient, as it uses so little coolant compared to other, contemporary systems.

Ensure the coolant level is topped up in the header tank, and that it has the correct percentage of anti-freeze (green in colour): you can check the mix with the aid of a hydrometer. Also check the condition of hoses, some of which use modern sprung clips that can easily fail and are often replaced with conventional jubilee clips.

If the 'low coolant' light on the dashboard illuminates (activated by a low coolant temperature sensor in the base of the header tank) it's important to check the coolant level immediately, as the 'comfort' temperature gauge on the dashboard is ineffective compared to the older temperature-controlled gauges.

Listen for the cooling fan coming on and staying on for an inordinate amount of time, indicating that the engine is over-heating. This can be caused by failure of the thermostat. The thermostat housing has plastic components that can stress, causing the hoses to blow off, leaking coolant and leading to over-heating. Aftermarket aluminium housings are now available, which can alleviate this problem.

Many earlier cooling systems suffer from failing water pumps as the plastic impellers break up over time, causing the engine to overheat and leading to inevitable problems. Later, Jaguar fitted pumps of an improved design, identified by the two-part pump body being bolted together. The easy way to identify a problem with earlier pumps is: with a cold engine, remove the filler cap from the expansion tank, start the engine, running it at around 1200rpm, and if the pump is working correctly, you'll see a constant swirl of coolant. The later, better coolant pumps are becoming expensive to buy so do make this check.

Water pumps are prone to failure.

The radiators and air-conditioning condensers are prone to collecting debris from the front, and impeding airflow and cooling ability. Many cars will not have had any work carried out here, but a cursory look from underneath will reveal the extent of any build-up of debris and/or damage to the cooling pack. It's strongly recommended that radiators are removed and flushed through thoroughly, from the inside and outside, with a high pressure jet at least every two years, to maintain cooling efficiency. This is something of a major job; to remove the radiator you need to remove the bonnet and disconnect the air-conditioning.

An easy way to check the efficiency of the water pump, from the swirl into the header tank.

Gearbox

No factory production XK8 or XKR models were fitted with a manual gearbox. All the automatic gearboxes are very reliable, but, just like an engine, require regular oil and filter changes, despite the fact that Jaguar identified them as 'sealed for life' and non-serviceable!

The ZF 5-speed gearbox fitted to the normally-aspirated 4.0-litre XK8 models has a forward clutch pack with a retaining clip that wears through the steel housing, eventually dropping out. A symptom of this is gear slipping, or, when hot, the gearbox temporarily not engaging until the revs are raised, when the gear then engages with a thump. Such a symptom, however, could also be due to a clogged filter, but whatever the reason, this isn't normal and requires investigation.

The Mercedes gearbox (4.0-litre XKR models only) also has its problems. The output shaft assemblies and planetary gears break up due to the earlier 'boxes having an aluminium housing that provided little support. This causes the gearbox to lock up and, as with the ZF, debris in the oil will clog the filter.

Therefore, it's vital that if any of these symptoms are found, the oil and filter are changed. Ideally, this is a standard practice service procedure at 60,000 and 80,000 mile intervals. A precise procedure (differing with each gearbox) must be followed to check the oil levels, and the procedure to change the oil and filter is also dependent on the type of gearbox and is quite involved. Even the oil is special (and costly!), so if you've any doubts about the gearbox, it's another good negotiating point.

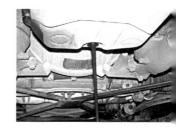

In many cases XK gearbox oil hasn't been changed in years.

The later 4.2-litre 6-speed gearboxes have proved little trouble but will benefit from the regular oil changes that aren't in the Jaguar service schedule. These gearboxes are remarkably smooth in operation, and if not, this is a good indication that an oil/filter change is necessary. The filter is an inclusive part of the plastic sump, so needs to be completely replaced each time the oil is changed.

Suspension/steering   4 3 2 1

The complex nature of the front subframe and its position make it vulnerable to damage.

The front suspension subframe is worth a more detailed inspection. Of high quality construction it doesn't suffer from corrosion, but can be vulnerable to damage. It's an extremely costly item to replace if damaged, and cannot be repaired.

It's important to note that if there are any creaks coming from the front suspension, it's possible that the top wishbone bushes have corroded sufficiently to bind the fulcrum pin. This means that (a) there's a risk that the suspension is worn where the fulcrum pin passes through (checked by jacking the car and evaluating the play at the top wishbone assembly), or (b) at the very least, the wishbone bush will have corroded into both the wishbone and the fulcrum pin – which probably means the fulcrum pin has corroded into the subframe, too. These can be extremely difficult to remove, and sometimes necessitate complete removal of the subframe. Look for rust around the top wishbone bushes, or rusting/damp areas bleaching out at the point the wishbone passes through. Does it appear that the wishbone has been forced into the bush? This is all indicative of the above problem, now very common on these cars.

Worn wishbone bushes (top), and the new replacements.

Also check the lower wishbone arm, which is an integral unit with the ball joint, and is very expensive to replace (these can be refurbished, but specialist equipment is needed).

Listen for front wheel bearing problems, evident by a constant drone (and often felt through the steering wheel) accentuated when the steering wheel is turned. If evident, the bearings need to be replaced immediately. Because of the pressure used to remove the wheel bearings, and because it requires special tools, this is not particularly a DIY job.

Returning to the front subframe, this is held onto the body via four mounts. The two round ones at the front cause very little problem, but the two V-mounts at the

Wheel bearing corrosion can be costly to repair.

rear locate on top of the subframe, and underneath the front chassis leg. A sandwich mount of aluminium-rubber-aluminium, they debond, giving the handling at the front a 'floating' feel. A long bolt passes through each V-mount into the chassis frame: this can be extremely difficult to remove, often shearing and then requiring the removal of the whole subframe to rectify.

Also at the front, check the power steering cooler, as this regularly fails. It's not difficult to replace, but there's a high pressure union that, again, requires a special tool. The power steering system isn't prone to leaks, so any that are identified may need remedial work.

Early models (pre-2000 model year) were fitted with a steering column prone to pronounced wear around the mid-point. It's a thick, round column with a grey gaiter situated about one-third of the way down, towards the steering rack. Wear is indicated by a knocking felt through the column. Rectification is by replacement with the later, substantially improved column – an expensive item!

At the rear there are two concerns. One is defective shock absorbers, identified by an inconsistent rumbling sound from the rear of the car over certain road surfaces. Replacement requires the unbolting and lowering of the entire rear suspension, and a special spring compressor.

The other concern is a slight leak from the pinion seal (where the propshaft is connected to the differential). To replace the pinion requires a substantial socket as this can be very tight, and the purchase of a complete seal and pinion assembly – quite costly.

Many cars were equipped with the Jaguar CATS active suspension system, and each shock absorber (front and rear) had an electrical connection to the main wiring loom. As the shock absorbers 'rotate' in service, these wires can eventually dislodge and break, bringing up a warning message on the dashboard. At the rear, this could necessitate the lowering of the entire suspension unit to fit new wiring.

A cursory glance underneath the car can soon identify any leaks.

The rear A-frame bushes rarely wear with age, but

Grit in the rear A-frame bushes.

when they do, they will cause knocks and bumps from the rear, so check them. In particular, check they are fitted with an appropriate adhesive, or they will move in service. A much more common issue relating to these knocks and bumps (or, at worst, a screeching noise) is gravel caught in the rear frame, but this can be easily removed, alleviating the problem.

The easy way to check if the car has CATS suspension: electrical connections to the turrets in the engine bay.

Brakes

4 3 2 1

If you've already checked the condition of the discs, and that the brakes operate satisfactorily, there isn't much else to worry about. Remember that brake discs rarely last more than 30,000 miles, because drivers tend to use their bakes more, and harder pad materials are used. Check the discs for smoothness and corrosion at the edges, and that the pads are in good condition.

R-Performance discs and pads are significantly more expensive to replace.

From the Road Test you should have already noticed the presence of any juddering or pulsating through the brake pedal, pulling to one side, or greater pedal travel, all of which can mean new pads and discs. The much bigger and more efficient Brembo braking system, for the XKR models (and now fitted to some other examples), can be very costly to maintain so always have some extra money in your budget for later service work.

The earlier cars' brake pipes are now corroding, so these should be closely inspected. Areas of major concern (necessitating them all being replaced) are: the front pipes leading down from the brake accumulator assembly (front-left of the engine bay), which corrode unseen, collecting debris from the front of the car; and the under floor pipes front-to-back of the vehicle, also prone to road debris. Another area of unseen pipe corrosion is behind the wheelarch splash-guards, where the pipes meet the caliper flexible hoses.

The handbrake, a cross-over from the previous XJ-S model, is renowned for poor adjustment, and replacing a cable necessitates removal of the one-piece carpeting inside the car.

Check all brake and fuel lines for corrosion.

Exhaust/wheels and tyres

4 3 2 1

Many XKs have now been fitted with modified exhaust systems, usually to create a more vibrant sound or to enhance gas flow and aid performance/economy. Nearly all are stainless steel, with varying degrees of quality and fit. Check the condition and the fit: does it look a professional job? How does it sound? Some create a booming and vibration at certain speeds which can be uncomfortable on long journeys.

Jaguar produced around 20 different alloy wheel designs for these cars. If equipped with the larger 19in and 20in wheels, the car should be fitted with rubber rear wheelarch extensions. These were an obligatory measure to meet construction and use regulations, as

A considerable number of XKs now have aftermarket exhaust systems fitted.

Rubber wheelarch extensions should always be fitted with the bigger rear wheels.

the wheels protrude slightly beyond the leading edge of the body.

Alloy wheels tend to 'stick' to the hubs due to galvanic action, so they should always be refitted with the aid of copper grease, which forms a natural barrier and enables the wheels to be removed easily (another sign of good care and maintenance).

Ensure the car sits evenly and squarely on the road.

Overall stance

4 3 2 1

XKs should sit square on the road, with no height difference front-to-rear. Overall ride height will vary according to the wheels and tyres fitted, and slight differences are detectable with differing suspension set-ups.

Bodywork panels and paintwork

4 3 2 1

XKs were well made and reasonably well protected, but, bear in mind that the earliest models now date back to 1996, so it's inevitable that some areas will be suspect. Apart from the items covered in the Fifteen Minute Evaluation, it's a simple matter of checking the overall view of the car, ensuring panels fit well, and there are no dents or scuffs to mar a good finish to the paintwork.

Like any other car, XK bodywork can corrode, so look at common areas like wheelarch lips, sills, rear wing to bumper, and any chips around the

Minor corrosion in an older car is normal and not a major issue.

door edges, fuel filler cap, and door handles. Stone chips and pebble rash are the most common areas of concern, which in many cases can necessitate a complete repaint of panels. Any previous respray work can usually be easily identified as the styling and general curvature of the body will show minute changes in colour.

Glass and wipers

The windscreen can suffer from minor scratches caused by the operation of the wipers against road grime. Jaguar dealerships used to polish the screens with a paste at regular services, but this practice has long gone. The wipers are effective and operate at two speeds (intermittent or auto cycle), controlled from the steering wheel-mounted stalk which also controls the screen wash system built into the wiper arms. Very little trouble is experienced with this system, but the wiper blades are rarely changed – except when they've caused significant screen damage.

Windscreens can be expensive to replace, particularly if graduated-tinted or heated.

Check for obvious stone chip damage or cracks to the windscreen as this is a costly item to replace, particularly if equipped with a heated element. If so equipped, check that it works. The door windows are also prone to scratching, and it's not unknown for the edges to be chipped, as the doors are frameless. On Convertible models check the grip of the windows within the doors (when raised). Doors are often slammed with the windows up, causing a slackening of the glass in the frame.

Normally-aspirated front nose detail.

Body trim

There's very little external brightwork on XK models, and what chrome there is, is plated onto plastic for lightness and longevity.

At the front, normally-aspirated cars have a chromed crossbar in the air intake with two vertically-mounted plastic overriders supporting the registration plate. Black finishers around the crossbar direct air into the 'mouth' to the radiator, so check these are not damaged or missing. On supercharged models a stainless mesh grille is used instead of the crossbar, which should be checked for dents and other damage.

On the earlier models in particular, the front bumper under-valance area gets damaged from road and kerb contact, sometimes being ripped off entirely. The 'tongue' in the middle of the valance should ideally be cable-tied to the front suspension cross-brace or

anti-roll bar. Check that this under-valance is intact as it can affect airflow to the engine area.

Many owners have changed the mounting of the front registration plate, in some cases using a stick-on type across the nose, above the mouth (where the growler badge usually sits). There is some question about the legality of this, due to the angle of sight from a distance. It's worth considering this, as to remove the plate and re-position it will probably require repainting of the nose section.

Non-standard fitment of a front registration plate.

Except for US spec models and aftermarket fitment, screen trims are in painted grey finish and door handles match the body colour. US spec models had chrome finish to both, including the door-mounted, rear view mirrors (push-fit chromed caps for these could be purchased as an accessory from Jaguar). Condition should be good in all these areas, as the window surrounds, for example, are difficult to remove and not worth repainting, as replacements are readily available.

For the 2004 model year the sill areas gained over-sill covers, so check the condition of these.

HID lighting units are very expensive to repair and replace.

Lighting

Check that all exterior lighting works. Some later model's headlights may be Xenon (HID) charged gas types, which should operate quickly, but note any deterioration in the lighting. These are very expensive to replace, with each headlight having its own control unit sitting underneath, and can suffer from water ingress. If, when turning on the lights, the bulb doesn't illuminate and the headlight bulk (not the main beam bulb) doesn't rise and fall, this indicates a fault with the circuit board: the only solution is replacement. Conventional headlights use normal bulbs, but any cracks in the outer glass will necessitate a complete change of the light unit. All XKs suffer from a build-up of condensation within the headlight units, which could be improved by a modification recommended by Jaguar Cars that provided venting, but this isn't fitted to many cars.

Front side lights are an inclusive part of the front light units and, again, have replaceable bulbs (as do the indicator units). Integrated fog lights are a feature of all cars, inset on the earlier examples, and flush-mounted from around 2001. They're vulnerable to stone damage and water ingress so

Front auxiliary lights are vulnerable.

Late chrome surround rear lights fit differently: if on an earlier car, check for internal wing damage, and neat wiring.

check they're intact and operational. To replace, if the inserts 'spin,' it may be necessary to remove the whole bumper assembly.

At the rear, the light clusters give little trouble, again all with interchangeable bulb fitting. Later models have a revised light unit incorporating a chrome surround. Many owners have adapted these to fit the earlier cars but this involved some degree of re-wiring and altering the interior framework of the rear wings.

All XK lighting is controlled by quite expensive lamp modules, and any problems usually show themselves via warning indicators on the dashboard. Such problems can either be sorted very easily (loose wires, connections, etc), or expensively (by the replacement of modules).

Bonnet and boot

[4] [3] [2] [1]

Underside paint finishes are matt, compared to exterior panel shine.

Under-bonnet and other hidden areas of bodywork will be finished in a slightly lighter, matt colour finish compared to exterior panels. This is normal, due to the paint process applied. If conventional high-gloss paint (or over-spray) is found in these areas, it's a sure sign of remedial body and paintwork having been carried out.

The boot area is usually completely trouble free, but removing the carpeted floorpanels will reveal the general condition in this area. Look for damage which may have been caused by rear end impact, and ensure all the electrics are intact, tidy, and damp free.

Earlier cars didn't have a separate external boot button, relying on an electric release from the dashboard or the use of a key in the boot lock. Later models are equipped with a chrome finisher above the registration plate area which contains a push button to open the boot. Some owners have now fitted the later system to earlier cars, which required some re-wiring, so it's worth checking for any unsightly wiring inside the boot indicating the change hadn't been carried out professionally.

Later model with external boot release button and chromed finisher.

Signs of previous floorpan corrosion.

Simply peeling back the front inner wing rubber closing panel can reveal hidden corrosion.

Underside, sills and floors

④ ③ ② ①

The front inner wings are protected by pre-formed rubber closing panels held in place by self-tapping screws. Ideally these should be removed for a closer inspection of the inner wheelarches where corrosion often forms, hidden from view. Such areas are often forgotten and really need wax protection, as the closing panels rarely seal out all the damp.

The XK floorpan is a carry-over from the XJ-S, with adaptations to suit the different drive train, and is therefore a vulnerable area if not well protected. The most important issue is corrosion under the front footwells where a double-skinned plate lies. This will corrode and crack, and is highly visible from underneath the car. It's not uncommon to be able to touch the interior carpeting through corrosion holes found underneath the car! You can't identify the problem from inside the car because of the one-piece moulded carpet. However, if corrosion has taken hold it will allow damp into the car beneath the carpet, which will spread and eventually rust out the whole floorpan.

Another problem area is the rear chassis legs, as they rise up following the inside line of the rear wheelarches (forward of the rear axle). Two pieces of metal fold over to form the box section, and the seams are easily visible with the rear wheels removed; they're prone to water ingress, swelling and cracking. The right-hand side is more easily repairable, even with the

Behind the front inner wing closing panels is a maze of pipework and areas that can rust out.

Rear chassis leg area.

axle in situ, but for the left-hand repair, matters are more complex because of the lie of the fuel lines.

The rear inner wings are more vulnerable because they don't have closing panels to protect them. Body colour painted from new, they also received a hand brushed black finish before assembly, but this was ineffective against the ravages of winter driving so it's an area to check out, even if it means removing the rear road wheels to investigate further.

Any floorpan/sill join area repairs are likely to be expensive to put right, not least because they require the removal of all interior trim in the area.

Fuel tank and pipework

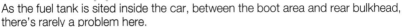

As the fuel tank is sited inside the car, between the boot area and rear bulkhead, there's rarely a problem here.

Fuel lines can be an issue, and need replacement, particularly if the rear underside fuel filter isn't changed regularly, as it should be. Joints become tight, corrosion sets in, and a bigger job than a normal service can result!

Roof

The Coupé models have no problems other than paintwork issues. Convertible hoods should be checked for condition, both inside and out, as they're very expensive to buy and replace. Colour and water repellency can be rejuvenated with specialist materials, but severe scuffs or tears cannot. The rear window is glass and has an electric heating element, so check that it works, and also that the window seal is intact and not leaking. The hoods aren't prone to leaks, but, in heavy rain with the front windows open, water may stream in, penetrating the carpet and helping to feed corrosion in the floorpan. Replacement hood seals should be checked for creasing and distortion, as they're expensive to replace.

Hoods are very expensive to replace.

The electrically controlled hydraulic hood mechanism should work smoothly, and take 18-25 seconds to cycle through. Ensure it works correctly, looking for the following after holding down the hood button:
• The front door windows retract approximately 2in.
• The rear quarter windows retract fully.
• The hood latch mechanism to the screen unlatches.
• The hood unfurls into its well.
• A bleep signals the completion of the operation.

Ensure the hood mechanism performs smoothly and within a reasonable time.

All the Convertibles have a separate leather hood cover, that clips into position over the hood to protect it from road grime. This should have its own black sleeve to retain it in the boot. If either are missing, negotiate!

The cycle to erect the hood from the down position should be as follows:
• The screen-mounted latch releases.
• If raised, the door windows lower approximately 2in.
• The hood raises smoothly.
• The hood connects at the top of the screen, with the latch and lock.
• The rear quarter windows raise fully.
• The front door windows raise fully.
• A bleep signals the completion of the operation.

Many of the early hood mechanisms suffered from congealing fluid, requiring purging and replacement with a revised fluid, CHF 11S. Any hesitation in the hood mechanism should be investigated.

The correct (later) fluid for Convertible hydraulics.

Classic interior finish, with full leather and walnut veneer ...

... special edition carbon fibre interior ...

... and later Piano Black interior.

Cabin trim

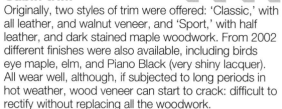

Originally, two styles of trim were offered: 'Classic,' with all leather, and walnut veneer, and 'Sport,' with half leather, and dark stained maple woodwork. From 2002 different finishes were also available, including birds eye maple, elm, and Piano Black (very shiny lacquer). All wear well, although, if subjected to long periods in hot weather, wood veneer can start to crack: difficult to rectify without replacing all the woodwork.

Leather and cloth trim lasts well, although the driver's seat bolster inevitably suffers. Minor cracks and scuffs can easily be addressed with modern techniques, and most used XKs that passed through the franchised dealerships were subjected to remedial upholstery treatment at some point. The later seats, with separate headrests, seem to wear better, and cushion sagging is rarely a problem with any model. Some cars were equipped with Recaro seating, providing better lateral support; they were more expensive fitted from new, and may affect the price of a car you're considering buying.

Minor trim is rarely a problem, although the centre console armrest area can suffer from scuffing and discolouration, as can the 'cheeks' around the side of the centre console, and the under dash panels.

The veneered trim around the gear selector lever is prone to damage, and the plastic surround to the gear selector is often lose and cracked. Some of the door trim clips are 'one use only,' and should ideally have been replaced if this area has been tampered with. Check that everything fits flush and neat, and that there are no unsightly marks or scuffs to any of the upholstery.

Look for minor damage like this, which suggests someone has 'been there before,' rectifying problems.

Instruments and electrics

Any messages on the dashboard should be thoroughly investigated.

Assuming all the checks were carried out during the Road Test and the Fifteen Minute Evaluation, it's again worth checking that all the switches and gauges work properly.

Start with the electric window controls. The doors are frameless, so the glass windows 'bite' into elaborate rubber seals, forming a totally draught- and noise-free seal. When opening the doors, the windows automatically retract about 2in, and raise again into the seal upon closing. If the vehicle's electrics have been disconnected, or the battery is failing, this process doesn't work; but it's a simple matter to reset, and worth doing to ensure the problem is not more involved.

If previously checked, but later the windows don't work properly, assess battery condition.

Sitting in the driver's seat, press the driver's window button, keeping it depressed until the glass has fully retracted. Continue holding it for a few seconds, until you hear an audible 'click,' then release the button. Then, raise the window fully, again holding the button in until you hear another 'click.' You should now be able to fully lower or raise the glass with a single touch: the glass should retract 2in when opening the door, and then raise into the seals when closing the door. Repeat the same procedure for the passenger door, and all should work normally – if not, more serious investigation is needed.

The electrically operated door mirrors are controlled by the rotary switch on the driver's door trim. Some models are also equipped with a fold-back facility (if so equipped, check that this works). Similarly, memory seat adjustment is fitted (either to only the driver's door, or both doors), and can be checked by adjusting the seat to a particular position, pressing M1, moving the seat manually, and then pressing M1 again to see if the seat moves back into position.

Multi-functioning switchgear on the steering wheel should be checked for operation.

Some models are equipped with electric steering wheel adjustment, controlled via a switch on the side of the steering column. Check this works when set to 'Auto:' the column should adjust as you enter and exit the car, inserting or removing the key in the ignition. Cars may also be equipped with steering wheel mounted controls for the audio system, and cruise control – check that these functions work.

Check that all interior lighting works, and notice, in particular, the centre

A seemingly minor matter, like switch illumination, can be problematic.

console area, which is prone to problems with the lighting, auxiliary switching, and radio functions. Whilst not difficult to replace, bulbs (there are up to a dozen of them) can be surprisingly expensive: they're specialist bulbs, each of which must be fitted into its correct place, and it can be a fiddly job, removing the console trim, wood surround, etc.

Look for any warning lights on the dashboard, which should be investigated. Common areas of concern are the ABS/traction control warning lights, which, at worst, could mean repairing or replacing the ABS module under the bonnet at considerable expense. A car will fail an MoT test with either of these warnings present. There's also a 'limp home' mode, which restricts performance when the system detects a problem. In many cases this can simply be due to a loose wire, but in others it can be major issue, so beware if this happens during your evaluation.

ABS modules are expensive to replace, although they can now be repaired.

All XKs are equipped with air-conditioning, and this should work quietly and quickly to bring down the temperature. It's worth trying the system at various temperature settings to ensure it works efficiently.

On pre-2003 models, it's possible to carry out a basic diagnostics check yourself, by pressing the 'Auto' and 'Recirculating' buttons simultaneously, while you restart the system. The panel display flashes, and the system enters diagnostics mode. Pressing 'Auto' again will display either a zero, or one of several error codes. You can cycle through these by using the 'Demist' button. The easiest code to diagnose is '23,' meaning low refrigerant, a common problem, which prevents the compressor from engaging. You cannot replenish the refrigerant yourself, as this requires specialist equipment. The compressor, however, may not work for other reasons, and, if so, this could mean the replacement of this quite expensive unit.

On later models, it's not possible to carry out in-car diagnostics checks like this; they require the full diagnostic equipment as used by franchised dealers and some specialist independents. Overall, it's best to ensure the system works before you buy the car!

Finally, check auxiliary equipment. Many cars were equipped with the Premium Sound System, providing hi-fi quality sound. This system included tweeter (high frequency) speakers built into the forward edge of the doors, and extra bass speaker(s) built into the rear compartment (different on Coupé and Convertible models), plus extra amplification. Check that it's fully operational, as damaged speakers are expensive unless you buy cheaper, non-Jaguar, aftermarket types. Similarly, the CD auto-changer fitted in the boot should have a magazine to hold upto 6 CDs, so check it's present: insert some CDs and ensure it selects and plays them properly.

Does every gadget on the car work?

Some later models also had an integrated satellite navigation system, with a dashboard-mounted screen replacing the central auxiliary gauges and clock (a clock now incorporated into the sat-nav screen). This system generally works without

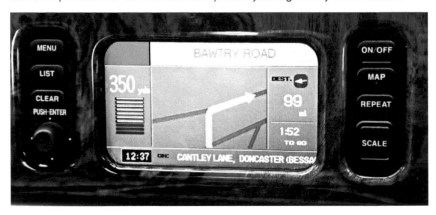

Satellite navigation, because of its age, shouldn't warrant a price premium.

Is the battery in good condition, and is it the correct size and power for the XK?

issues, but the price of the car should not be dictated by this addition. It's an old system and is no longer supported, so, other than getting some later disks via the internet, it's not a system you can update regularly.

Other extra cost equipment available on the XKs included cruise control, adaptive cruise control (which tracked the car's forward distance from other vehicles and adjusted the speed accordingly), and speed regulated control, restricting the car's speed to a predetermined limit. Again, check all these functions work correctly if fitted.

As with any modern car, the condition of the battery is crucial to the way the car operates, and the XK is no exception. Modern batteries have an extended life-span, but once they deteriorate to a certain level, they 'die' instantly, and can't be reinvigorated by charging. Don't attempt to jump start one of these cars from another vehicle whilst the 'donor' vehicle's engine is running; this can cause a major electrical spike, resulting in undeterminable damage to the XK's electronics. So beware of a car that has a 'duff' battery.

Miscellaneous checks [4] [3] [2] [1]

The following little things are worth checking, otherwise extra costs (sometimes larger than you think) are likely.

Are there two sets of keys and key fobs? Do both key fobs operate the alarm and immobiliser system? If not, they'll need re-programming with a Jaguar diagnostics system; quite expensive! If the batteries in a key fob are dead, they must be changed within ten minutes, or the vital link to the car is lost, and the fob will require reprogramming.

Does the radio aerial rise and fall smoothly when the audio system is turned on? If not, it hasn't been lubricated!

Is all the paperwork with the car? Handbook, maintenance handbook, service record book, security booklet, extra equipment handbooks (eg satellite navigation, audio systems) and, not least, the lovely leather folder for the glove box, and the black plastic folder for the service data, that fits in the boot.

And finally, recheck the boot for all the tools, especially the locking wheel nut key.

Do both of the key fobs work?

Evaluation procedure

Add up the total points score: 72 = excellent; 54 = good; 36 = average; 18 = buyer beware! Cars scoring over 50 should be completely usable and require the minimum of repair or rectification, although continued service maintenance and care will be required to keep them in good condition. Cars scoring between 18 and 37 will require serious work (at much the same cost regardless of score). Cars scoring between 38 and 49 will require very careful assessment of the necessary repair costs in order to reach a realistic re-sale value in future.

10 Auctions
– sold! Another way to buy your dream

Auctions are a good source of XK8 and XKR models, providing you take sufficient care over your intended purchase.

Auctions can provide a bargain if you're careful.

Auction pros & cons
Pros: Prices are usually lower than those of dealers or private sellers and you might grab a real bargain on the day. Auctioneers have usually established clear title with the seller. At the venue you can usually examine documentation relating to the vehicle.

Cons: You have to rely on a sketchy catalogue description of condition and history. The opportunity to inspect is limited and you cannot drive the car. Auction cars are often a little below par and may require some work. It's easy to overbid. There will usually be a buyer's premium to pay in addition to the auction hammer price.

Which auction?
Auctions by established auctioneers are advertised in car magazines and on the auction houses' websites. A catalogue, or a simple printed list of the lots for

auctions might only be available a day or two ahead, though often lots are listed and pictured on auctioneers' websites much earlier. Contact the auction company to ask if previous auction selling prices are available as this is useful information (details of past sales are often available on websites).

Catalogue, entry fee and payment details

When you purchase the catalogue of the vehicles in the auction, it often acts as a ticket allowing two people to attend the viewing days and the auction. Catalogue details tend to be comparatively brief, but will include information such as 'one owner from new, low mileage, full service history,' etc. It will also usually show a guide price to give you some idea of what to expect to pay and will tell you what is charged as a 'Buyer's premium.' The catalogue will also contain details of acceptable forms of payment. At the fall of the hammer an immediate deposit is usually required, the balance payable within 24 hours. If the plan is to pay by cash there may be a cash limit. Some auctions will accept payment by debit card. Sometimes credit or charge cards are acceptable, but will often incur an extra charge. A bank draft or bank transfer will have to be arranged in advance with your own bank as well as with the auction house. No car will be released before all payments are cleared. If delays occur in payment transfers then storage costs can accrue.

Buyer's premium

A buyer's premium will be added to the hammer price: don't forget this in your calculations. It is not usual for there to be a further state tax or local tax on the purchase price and/or on the buyer's premium.

Viewing

In some instances it's possible to view on the day, or days before, as well as in the hours prior to, the auction. There are auction officials available who are willing to help out by opening engine and luggage compartments and to allow you to inspect the interior. While the officials may start the engine for you, a test drive is out of the question. Crawling under and around the car as much as you want is permitted, but you can't suggest that the car you are interested in be jacked up, or attempt to do the job yourself. You can also ask to see any documentation available.

Bidding

Before you take part in the auction, decide your maximum bid – and stick to it!

It may take a while for the auctioneer to reach the lot you are interested in, so use that time to observe how other bidders behave. When it's the turn of your car, attract the auctioneer's attention and make an early bid. The auctioneer will then look to you for a reaction every time another bid is made, usually the bids will be in fixed increments until the bidding slows, when smaller increments will often be accepted before the hammer falls. If you want to withdraw from the bidding, make sure the auctioneer understands your intentions – a vigorous shake of the head when he or she looks to you for the next bid should do the trick!

Assuming that you are the successful bidder, the auctioneer will note your card or paddle number, and from that moment on you will be responsible for the vehicle.

If the car is unsold, either because it failed to reach the reserve or because there was little interest, it may be possible to negotiate with the owner, via the auctioneers, after the sale is over.

Successful bid

There are two more items to think about. How to get the car home, and insurance. If you can't drive the car, your own or a hired trailer is one way, another is to have the vehicle shipped using the facilities of a local company. The auction house will also have details of companies specialising in the transfer of cars.

Insurance for immediate cover can usually be purchased on site, but it may be more cost-effective to make arrangements with your own insurance company in advance, and then call to confirm the full details.

eBay & other online auctions

eBay and other online auctions could land you a car at a bargain price, though you'd be foolhardy to bid without examining the car first, something most vendors encourage. A useful feature of eBay is that the geographical location of the car is shown, so you can narrow your choices to those within a realistic radius of home. Be prepared to be outbid in the last few moments of the auction. Remember, your bid is binding and that it will be very, very difficult to get restitution in the case of a crooked vendor fleecing you – caveat emptor!

Be aware that some cars offered for sale in online auctions are 'ghost' cars. Don't part with any cash without being sure that the vehicle does actually exist and is as described (usually pre-bidding inspection is possible).

Auctioneers

Barrett-Jackson: www.barrett-jackson.com.
Bonhams: www.bonhams.com
British Car Auctions (BCA): www.bca-europe.com or www.british-car-auctions.co.uk
Cheffins: www.cheffins.co.uk
Christies: www.christies.com
Coys: www.coys.co.uk
eBay: www.eBay.com
H&H: www.classic-auctions.co.uk
RM: www.rmauctions.com
Shannons: www.shannons.com.au
Silver: www.silverauctions.com

A lot of paperwork and information came with new Jaguars: is it still available?

Classic, collector and prestige cars usually come with a large portfolio of paperwork accumulated and passed on by a succession of proud owners. This documentation represents the real history of the car and from it can be deduced the level of care the car has received, how much it's been used, which specialists have worked on it and the dates of major repairs and restorations. All of this information will be priceless to you as the new owner, so be very wary of cars with little paperwork to support their claimed history.

Registration documents

All countries/states have some form of registration for private vehicles whether it's like the American 'pink slip' system or the British 'log book' system.

It is essential to check that the registration document is genuine, that it relates to the car in question, and that all the vehicle's details are correctly recorded, including chassis/VIN and engine numbers (if these are shown). If you are buying from the previous owner, his or her name and address will be recorded in the document: this will not be the case if you are buying from a dealer.

In the UK the current (Euro-aligned) registration document is named V5C, and is printed in coloured sections of blue, green and pink. The blue section relates to the car specification, the green section has details of the new owner and the pink section is sent to the DVLA in the UK when the car is sold. A small section in yellow deals with selling the car within the motor trade.

In the UK the DVLA will provide details of earlier keepers of the vehicle upon payment of a small fee, and much can be learned in this way.

If the car has a foreign registration there may be expensive and time-consuming formalities to complete. Do you really want the hassle?

Roadworthiness certificate

Most country/state administrations require that vehicles are regularly tested to prove that they are safe to use on the public highway and do not produce excessive emissions. In the UK that test (the 'MoT') is carried out at approved testing stations, for a fee. In the USA the requirement varies, but most states insist on an emissions test every two years as a minimum, while the police are charged with pulling over unsafe-looking vehicles.

In the UK the test is required on an annual basis once a vehicle becomes three years old. Of particular relevance for older cars is that the certificate issued includes the mileage reading recorded at the test date and, therefore, becomes an independent record of that car's history. Ask the seller if previous certificates are available. Without an MoT the vehicle should be trailered to its new home, unless you insist that a valid MoT is part of the deal. (Not such a bad idea this, as at least you will know the car was roadworthy on the day it was tested and you don't need to wait for the old certificate to expire before having the test done.)

Road licence

The administration of every country/state charges some kind of tax for the use of its road system, the actual form of the 'road licence,' and how it is displayed, varying enormously country to country and state to state.

Whatever the form of the 'road licence,' it must relate to the vehicle carrying it and must be present and valid if the car is to be driven on the public highway legally. The value of the license will depend on the length of time it will continue to be valid.

In the UK if a car is untaxed because it has not been used for a period of time, the owner has to inform the licensing authorities, otherwise the vehicle's date-related registration number will be lost and there will be a painful amount of paperwork to get it re-registered.

Certificates of authenticity

For many makes of collectible car it is possible to get a certificate proving the age and authenticity (eg engine and VIN/chassis numbers, paint colour and trim) of a particular vehicle, these are called 'Heritage Certificates' and in the case of the XK can be acquired from the Jaguar Heritage Trust in Coventry, UK. If the car comes with one of these it is a definite bonus. If you want to obtain one, contact the Trust via www.jdht.com

Valuation certificate

Hopefully, the vendor will have a recent valuation certificate, or letter signed by a recognised expert stating how much he, or she, believes the particular car to be worth (such documents, together with photos, are usually needed to get 'agreed value' insurance). Generally such documents should act only as confirmation of your own assessment of the car rather than a guarantee of value as the expert has probably not seen the car in the flesh. The easiest way to find out how to obtain a formal valuation is to contact the owners' club.

Previous ownership records
Due to the introduction of important new legislation on data protection, it is no longer possible to acquire, from the British DVLA, a list of previous owners of a car you own, or are intending to purchase. This scenario will also apply to dealerships and other specialists, from who you may wish to make contact and acquire information on previous ownership and work carried out.

Service history
Often, older cars will have been serviced at home by enthusiastic (and hopefully capable) owners for a good number of years. Nevertheless, try to obtain as much service history and other paperwork pertaining to the car as you can. Naturally, dealer stamps, or specialist garage receipts score most points in the value stakes. However, anything helps in the great authenticity game, items like the original bill of sale, handbook, parts invoices and repair bills, adding to the story and the character of the car. Even a brochure correct to the year of the car's manufacture is a useful document, and something that you could well have to search hard to locate in future years. If the seller claims that the car has been restored, then expect receipts and other evidence from a specialist restorer.

If the seller claims to have carried out regular servicing, ask what work was completed, when, and seek some evidence of it being carried out. Your assessment of the car's overall condition should tell you whether the seller's claims are genuine.

Restoration photographs
If the seller tells you that the car has been restored (or, more appropriately in the case of these quite modern cars, refurbished), then expect to be shown a series of photographs taken while the work was under way. Pictures taken at various stages, and from various angles, should help you gauge the thoroughness of the work. If you buy the car, ask if you can have all the photographs, as they form an important part of the vehicle's history. It's surprising how many sellers are happy to part with their car and accept your cash, but want to hang on to their photographs! In the latter event, you may be able to persuade the vendor to get a set of copies made.

12 What's it worth?
– let your head rule your heart

Condition

If the car you've been looking at is really bad, then you've probably not bothered to use the marking system in chapter 9 – '*60 minute evaluation.*' You may not have even got as far as using that chapter at all!

If you did use the marking system in chapter 9, you'll know whether the car is in Excellent (maybe Concours), Good, Average or Buyer Beware condition or, perhaps, somewhere in-between these categories.

Many car magazines run a regular price guide. If you haven't bought the latest issues, do so now and compare their suggested values for the model you are thinking of buying: also look at the auction prices they're reporting. Some models will always be more sought-after than others. Trends can change too. The published values tend to vary from one magazine to another, as do the scales of condition, so read the guidance notes carefully. Bear in mind that a car that is in truly magnificent condition or even a recent show winner, could be worth more than the highest scale published. Assuming the car you have in mind is not in show/Concours condition, then relate the level of condition that you judge the car to be in with the appropriate guide price. How does the figure compare with the asking price? Before you start haggling with the seller, consider what affect any variation from standard specification might have on the car's value.

If you are buying from a dealer, remember there will be a dealer's premium on the price.

There's plenty of XK price information, within both monthly magazines and in regular price guide books.

Desirable options/extras

These are additional options to standard equipment that might have been available when the car was new (at extra cost), or later modifications, as many are now available for these cars. In many cases these can still command a premium over cars without them.

Specific options that are beneficial and expensive to retro-fit are: cruise control (standard or adaptive, the latter only applicable to later models), CATS suspension system, a premium sound system with CD player, electrically adjustable steering wheel, and Xenon lighting.

New, extra cost options like these Recaro seats are still worth a premium.

XKs are quite 'colour sensitive.'

The majority of exterior paint finishes were metallic, so this shouldn't affect price, but, some colours are more popular than others, like blues, reds, and silver. Full leather interior is also desirable, as is walnut veneer, but prices are rarely affected.

All cars were equipped with alloy wheels and many cars were, or are now, equipped with the larger 19in or 20in split-rim alloys with low profile tyres. They look good, fill the wheelarches, but aren't cheap to refurbish, so if fitted, it's highly desirable to have them in excellent condition. Alloy wheels from the later XK model range (2006 on) will NOT fit these earlier models. A full-sized spare wheel is desirable, but not always practical, as the larger 19in and 20in will not fit in the bootwell area.

There has been a trend with XK owners for retro-fitting styling and exhaust enhancements. Only the very late XKR models had a four-pipe exhaust system, but owners can now fit specialised stainless steel systems with two or four, small or large bore pipes. The most common styling changes include fitting alloy mesh grilles to the mouth (similar, but not the same, as those on XKR models), lighting changes, and – one which is particularly useful – the fitting of a separate boot button lock to the earlier cars that only have a key lock or dash mounted release method.

Buyers like 'big' wheels: the early 17in Revolver wheels are the least desirable.

Some companies now offer electronic upgrades in the form of 'tweaked' ECUs and, in the case of supercharged models, larger pulleys to enhance the speed at which the supercharger turns, both of which can increase performance. But you should ensure they came from, and were fitted by, a bona fide source.

Undesirable features

XKs are colour sensitive (or their owners are!). White was never a popular colour, particularly in the cooler European climes, although it was very common in hot countries for obvious reasons. The early turquoise colour is an acquired taste, as are unusual darker colours, like Amaranth.

Some owners have personalised their cars with the addition of different colour schemes, revised trim, extra chrome, etc. Excellent for those who like such things, but as these are generally very personal, they can prove difficult to sell on.

As far as the standard interiors were concerned the early half leather trim and dark stained maple veneer of the Sports models are as unpopular today as they were when new. Similarly, there are hardly any XK8s left with the original 17in Revolver style wheels, as they are still considered too small for the car (and boring!).

LPG (liquid petroleum gas) is quite a common modification, and there are a number of XKs so adapted. Whilst they cut down the cost of running these cars, they do impinge on boot or spare wheel space, and as the cars are sporty by nature and tend to do less mileage than saloons, many long-term owners turn away from such changes as the cost isn't warranted.

Very few people go to extremes with these cars. Fitting manual transmissions, or extensively modifying engines, etc, is rare, and doesn't usually improve the car's practicality for normal road use; it may even prove troublesome over a period of time.

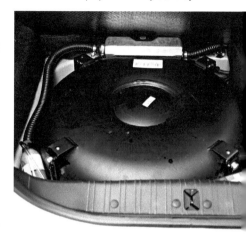

Liquid petroleum gas: not a common modification, although becoming more popular – but was it professionally installed?

Striking a deal

Negotiate on the basis of your condition assessment, mileage, and fault rectification cost. Also take into account the car's specification. Be realistic about the value, but don't be completely intractable: a small compromise on the part of the vendor or buyer will often facilitate a deal at little real cost.

13 Do you really want to restore?

– it'll take longer and cost more than you think

The XK models are not old enough to warrant restoration in the true sense of the term and, as there's a plentiful supply of cars at varying prices to suit everyone's needs, there seems little point in actually carrying out major refurbishment. The cost of the parts and labour required makes this prohibitive.

There are, also, numerous cars around that are available as Category D write-offs (cars that have been severely damaged beyond normal repair but which have been rebuilt and made roadworthy). The very nature of insurance claims, and the high labour costs of repairs to modern cars, makes it impractical for insurance companies to sanction such major repairs to many models. However, such 'projects' can be purchased quite cheaply, and subsequently repaired, but will always retain the Category D indication on the log sheet, so are usually much cheaper than other examples. If you want a cheap car, these can be worth considering – just remember you'll never get a reasonable price for such a car in re-sale.

Category D damaged cars can be rebuilt, or at worst supply a wealth of cheaper parts.

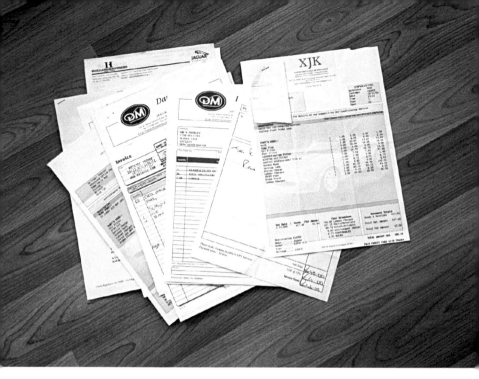

There should be no reason why a wealth of paperwork hasn't been accumulated to substantiate any work done.

Major work on an XK can be a daunting consideration for the uninitiated, or even a qualified mechanic, who may not be familiar with them, or used to such sophisticated modern vehicles. If you have never refurbished a car before, or even done major work on a more conventional (older) model, you're best avoiding an XK as a project. Specialist tools will be needed, and, in many cases, expensive replacement parts. Even franchised dealers, with their technically advanced diagnostic equipment, sometimes have to replace parts (at cost to the owner) in an attempt to cure faults, which sometimes doesn't work! DIY servicing is possible, but other work needs serious consideration, and a deep budget.

The one advantage is that Jaguar produced a lot of these cars, and many have already been dismantled. With current legislation, dismantling is an art in itself, and the authorised companies that carry out such work throw away hardly anything. They clean, refurbish, and test many items, and make them available for purchase – much cheaper than going to your Jaguar dealership, and they sometimes come with a warranty.

These cars wear well inside, so, it's unlikely that major work is required, although the soft leather on the driver's seat can suffer from constant scuffing. Upholstery repair specialists can work wonders, and there are many kits available that enable you to do the work yourself. New sets of wood veneer are also readily available aftermarket. Hoods are very expensive to replace, and the headlinings get dirty easily, so review them and take account of their condition when negotiating a price.

Paint faults generally occur due to lack of protection and/or maintenance, or to poor preparation prior to a respray or touch-up. Some of the following conditions may be present in the car you're looking at.

Accept that some remedial paintwork will have been carried out on most cars.

Orange peel

This appears as an uneven paint surface, similar to the appearance of the skin of an orange. The fault is caused by the failure of atomized paint droplets to flow into each other when they hit a surface. It's sometimes possible to rub out the effect with proprietary paint cutting/rubbing compound or very fine grades of abrasive paper. A respray may be necessary in severe cases. Consult a bodywork repairer/paint shop for advice on the particular car.

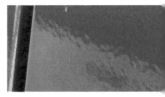

You may be able to rub out orange peel, but in severe cases a respray may be necessary.

Cracking

Severe cases are likely to have been caused by too heavy an application of paint (or filler beneath the paint). Also, insufficient stirring of the paint before application can lead to the components being improperly mixed, and cracking can result. Incompatibility with the paint already on the panel can have a similar effect. To rectify the problem it's necessary to rub down to a smooth, sound finish before respraying the problem area.

When does cracking become crazing? Both will require paint removal and respraying.

Crazing

Sometimes the paint takes on a crazed rather than a cracked appearance when the problems mentioned under 'Cracking' are present. This problem can also be caused by a reaction between the underlying surface and the paint. Paint removal and respraying the problem area is usually the only solution.

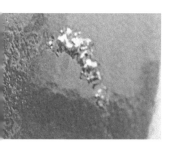

Blistering is almost always caused by corroded metal beneath the paint.

Blistering
Almost always caused by corrosion of the metal beneath the paint. Usually perforation will be found in the metal and the damage will usually be worse than that suggested by the area of blistering. The metal will have to be repaired before repainting.

Micro blistering
Usually the result of an economy respray where inadequate heating has allowed moisture to settle on the car before spraying. Consult a paint specialist, but usually damaged paint will have to be removed before partial or full respraying. Can also be caused by car covers that don't 'breathe.'

Fading
Some colours, especially reds, are prone to fading if subjected to strong sunlight for long periods without the benefit of polish protection. Sometimes proprietary paint restorers and/or paint cutting/rubbing compounds will retrieve the situation. Often a respray is the only real solution.

Peeling
Often a problem with metallic paintwork when the sealing lacquer becomes damaged and begins to peel off. Poorly applied paint may also peel. The remedy is to strip and start again!

Dimples
Dimples in the paintwork are caused by the residue of polish (particularly silicone types) not being removed properly before respraying. Paint removal and repainting is the only solution.

Dents
Small dents are usually easily cured by the 'Dentmaster,' or equivalent process, that sucks or pushes out the dent (as long as the paint surface is still intact). Companies offering dent removal services usually come to your home: consult your telephone directory.

Peeling paint occurs when the sealing lacquer becomes damaged: time to strip and start again.

15 Problems due to lack of use
– just like their owners XKs need exercise!

Cars, like humans, are at their most efficient if they exercise regularly. A run of at least twenty miles is needed just to thoroughly warm up a modern car like the XK, and good, regular use is strongly recommended.

Seized components
Pistons in brake calipers, slave and master cylinders can seize.

Handbrakes (parking brakes) can seize if the cables and linkages rust or are not lubricated, and the handbrake should be left off during long storage.

Fluids
Uninhibited coolant can corrode internal waterways. Lack of the correct mix of antifreeze in the coolant can severely damage an engine.

Silt settling and solidifying can cause overheating.

Brake fluid absorbs water from the atmosphere and should be renewed every two years. Old fluid with a high water content can cause corrosion and pistons/ calipers to seize (freeze), and can cause brake failure when the water turns to vapour near hot braking components,

Tyre problems
Tyres that have had the weight of the car on them in a single position for some time will develop flat spots, resulting in some (usually temporary) vibration. The tyre walls may also have cracks or (blister-type) bulges, meaning new tyres are needed. Tyres don't have an infinite life, even if the tread wear is low.

Modern alloy wheels can go 'oval' where a cars has been stored in the same position, long-term.

Shock absorbers (dampers)
With lack of use, the dampers will lose their elasticity or even seize. Creaking, groaning and stiff suspension are signs of this problem.

Rubber and plastic
Radiator hoses may have perished and split, possibly resulting in the loss of all coolant. Window and door seals can harden and leak. Gaitors/boots can crack. Wiper blades will harden.

Electrics
The battery will be of little use if it hasn't been charged for many months. These

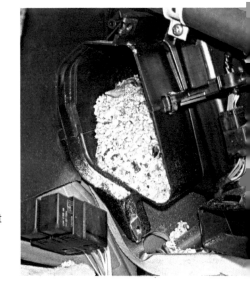

Rodent damage can be horrendous.

If long-term storage leads to any major electrical work being needed, this could be the amount of trim that has to be removed – very costly!

cars will always have a 'drain' from their electronics systems, which will slowly flatten the battery, unless a 'battery saver' device is fitted.

Earthing/grounding problems are common when the connections have corroded. Wiring insulation can harden and fail.

The modern electronic systems in the XK do not like lack of use.

Beware long-term storage in a country garage, where rodents can gain access. They have a habit of chewing electrical cables, or even storing their winter food in such diverse areas as air cleaners or air-conditioning systems.

Rotting exhaust system

Exhaust gas contains a high water content, so exhaust systems corrode very quickly from the inside when the car is not used. This even applies to stainless steel systems, internally and, in some cases, externally.

16 The Community
– key people, organisations and companies in the XK world

The XK8 and XKR have long been aspirational cars and still have a strong following. With so many produced over quite a long period, there are now examples to suit most pockets.

The franchised Jaguar dealer network still maintains many of these cars and is happy to continue looking after older examples. Jaguar Cars still supply the majority of parts required. There's now a strong network of independent Jaguar specialists who also maintain these vehicles, and spares businesses, already well known for the supply of parts for classic Jaguars, are now also catering for the XKs. There are also a few authorised dismantlers who can supply refurbished secondhand parts.

The cars are also very well supported by Jaguar marque clubs and internet sites, so there's ample opportunity to find out more from existing owners and seek advice when required. And finally, even though these cars are still relatively new, some insurance companies are already treating them as cherished vehicles, enabling owners to obtain reasonable car insurance.

Clubs

The Jaguar Drivers Club

18 Stuart Street, Luton, Bedfordshire LU1 2SL
Tel: +44 (0)1582 419332. www.jaguardriver.co.uk

The oldest of the Jaguar marque clubs, based in the UK, catering for all models with a monthly magazine, insurance scheme, and a good overseas network.

The Jaguar Enthusiasts Club

Abbeywood Office Park, Emma Chris Way, Filton, Bristol BS34 7JU
Tel: +4 (0)1179 698186. www.jec.org.uk

The world's largest Jaguar club, catering for all models with a special Forum and technical seminars for XK owners. 140-page full colour monthly magazine, insurance schemes, technical advice, specialist tools supply and hire plus events, tours and runs.

Jaguar Clubs of North America

C/o Nelson Rath, 1000 Glenbrook, Anchorage, KY 40223
Tel: +1 502 244 1672. www.jcna.com

The umbrella organisation for the US based Jaguar clubs with an events calendar and monthly magazine.

The XK8 Enthusiasts Club

2 Lynton Road South, Gravesend, Kent DA11 7NF
Tel: +44 (0)1474 354623. www.mark.gregory@xkec.co.uk

The newest and smallest of the UK based organisations, owned by an individual running a club specifically for the XK models, and with monthly magazine and regular events.

The Jaguar Heritage Trust

Jaguar Heritage Trust, c/o The Collections Centre, British Motor Museum, Banbury Road, Gaydon, Warwickshire CV35 OBJ
Tel: +44 (0)2476 401288. www.jdht.com
   Holder of the official Jaguar Cars archive, with information available on car build details, Heritage Certificate supply, CDs on service/maintenance information, plus photographic library.

Specialist independent XK service/maintenance providers:

David Marks Garages

Unit 36, Wilford & North Nottingham Industrial Estate, Ruddington Lane, Nottingham NG11 7EP
Tel: +44 (0)115 982 2808. www.davidmarksgarages.co.uk

R.G Bate (Engineering) Ltd

501 Cleveland Street, Birkenhead, Cheshire CH41 3EF
Tel: +44 (0)151 653 6765

Simon March & Co

Scoreby Lodge, Hull Road, Dunnington, York YO19 5LR
Tel: +44 (0)1904 489821

Winspeed Motorsport Ltd

148 Broad Street, Wood Street Village, Guildford, Surrey GU3 3BJ
Tel: +44 (0)1483 537706. www.winspeedmotorsport.com

Philip Welch Specialist Cars

Hull Road, Dunnington, York YO19 5LP
Tel: +44 (0)1904 488252 . www.philipwelch.co.uk

Nene Jag Specialists

8 Harvester Way, Fengate, Peterborough PE1 5UT
Tel: +44 (0)1733 349042 . www.nenejags.co.uk

Les Pauls Jaguar Specialists

Unit 7, Anderson Road Industrial Estate, Woodford Green, Essex IG8 8ET
Tel: +44 (0)208 551 8537 . www.lespauls.motors.co.uk

Parts suppliers

SNG Barratt Ltd

Stourbridge Road, Bridgnorth, Shropshire WV15 6AP
Tel: +44 (0)1746 765432. www.sngbarratt.com

Black Country Jaguars (refurbished parts)

Unit 5, The Hayes Business Park, The Hayes, Lye, Stourbridge DY9 8NR
Tel: +44 (0)1384 892121. www.blackcountryjaguar.com

Eurojag (refurbished parts)
Sovereign House, Neasham Road, Hurworth Moor, Darlington, County Durham DL2 1QH
Tel: +44 (0)1325 722777. www.eurojag.com

Modifications & upgrades
Adamesh
Unit 11, Acacia Close, Cherrycourt Way, Leighton Buzzard, Bedfordshire LU7 4QE
Tel: +44 (0)1525 852419. www.adamesh.co.uk

Racing Green Cars
Station Road West, Ashvale, Hampshire GU12 5QD
Tel: +44 (0)1252 544888. www.racinggreencars.com

Useful sources of information
Jaguar World Monthly magazine
The independent monthly magazine from Kelsey Publishing with regular features on these models.

You and Your Jaguar XK/XKR
By the author of this title, the all-in-one guide to the history and development of all the XK8 and XKR models including chapters on maintenance and modifications plus details specifications.

Jaguar Monthly XK8/XKR
Paperwork reprints of road test and other information previously found in issues of Jaguar Monthly magazine.

Jaguar – All the Cars, Veloce Publishing, ISBN: 978-1-845848-10-1
By the author of this title, the all-in-one guide to the history and development of all the Jaguar models with a special chapter on the X-350 models.

17 Vital statistics
– essential data at your fingertips

Production figures

XK8 4.0-litre Coupé	19,748	XKR 4.0-litre Coupé	9811
XK8 4.0-litre Convertible	46,770	XKR 4.0-litre Convertible	14,045

Technical specifications

Minor changes took place throughout the production period of the cars.
4.0-litre normally-aspirated engine: 3996cc 8 cylinder 32 valve DOHC 86mm x 86mm 290bhp @ 6100rpm & 290lb/ft @ 4250rpm.
4.0-litre supercharged engine 3996cc 8 cylinder 32 valve DOHC 86mm x 86mm 370bhp @ 6150rpm & 387lb/ft @ 3600rpm.
4.2-litre normally-aspirated engine: 4196cc 8 cylinder 32 valve DOHC 96mm x 90.3mm 300bhp @ 6000rpm & 310lb/ft @ 4100rpm.
4.2-litre supercharged engine: 4196cc 8 cylinder 32 valve DOHC 96mm x 90.3mm 400bhp @ 6100rpm & 408lb/ft @ 3500rpm.

Transmissions

4.0-litre normally-aspirated models: ZF 5-speed automatic with J-gate operation.
4.0-litre supercharged: Mercedes-Benz 5-speed automatic with J-gate operation.
4.2-litre (all models): ZF 6-speed automatic with J-gate operation.

Dimensions

Length: 187in (4750mm). Width: 72in (1829mm). Height: 51in (1295mm).
Weight: 3560lb (1615kg) (4.0-litre Coupé)
          3759lb (1705kg) (4.0-litre Convertible)
          3616lb (1640kg) (4.0-litre supercharged Coupé)
          3814lb (1730kg) (4.0-litre supercharged Convertible)
          3715lb (1685kg) (4.2-litre Coupé)
          3913lb (1775kg) (4.2-litre Convertible)
          3825lb (1735kg) (4.2-litre supercharged Coupé)
          4001lb (1815kg) (4.2-litre supercharged Convertible)

Suspension

Front: Independent unequal length wishbones, anti-dive, coil springs.
Rear: Independent double wishbones, drive shafts as upper links, anti-squat, coil springs.
CATS electronic control optional.

Brakes

Ventilated discs all round, power assisted with ABS.

Steering

Variable power assisted rack and pinion with adjustable steering wheel.

Wheels

17in (432mm) standard on 4.0-litre normally-aspirated models, with option of 18in (457mm).
18in (457mm) standard on 4.0-litre supercharged and all 4.2-litre models.
19in (483mm) and 20in (508mm) options for all cars.

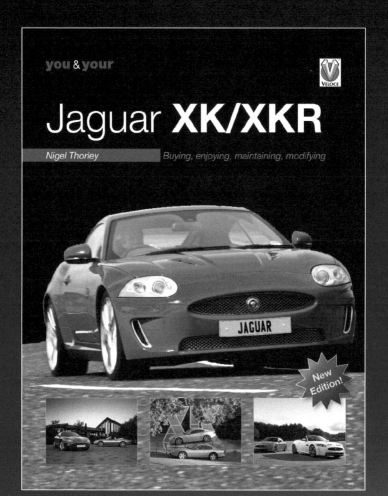

Index